# Little Talks: Big Feelings, Brave Words

For Kids Learning How to Feel, Speak, and Be Brave

by Aaron B Kershaw

# Little Talks: Big Feelings, Brave Words

## For Kids Learning How to Feel, Speak, and Be Brave

**Copyright © 2025 BuildingBlocs Publishing, Inc**
ISBN: 979-8-90345-029-9
**All Rights Reserved**



This manual is intended as a structural overview of the **Built from the Inside™** and **Pathlight™** systems. It is not a standalone implementation guide. The use of any system architecture, curriculum, session protocols, emotional tools, tier certifications, mentorship rubrics, or related training methods described herein, whether partial or complete, **requires an official licensing agreement through BuildingBlocs Academy** and **written authorization from BuildingBlocs Literacy LLC**.

The following are considered proprietary and are NOT included in this manual:

- The 10-book Built from the Inside™ and Pathlight™ participant series
- Facilitator coaching guides and certification scripts
- Tier-specific rubrics and evaluation templates
- Fidelity logs, escalation tools, and mentor certification exams
- Licensing frameworks, LMS access, and digital tracking tools
- BRIGHTPath™ trademarks, role graphics, and curriculum design IP

Unauthorized use, replication, adaptation, or institutional distribution of these proprietary tools or branded systems, whether commercial or nonprofit, may constitute intellectual property infringement and is strictly prohibited under U.S. and international copyright law.

For licensing, training, or implementation inquiries, contact the publisher:

**BuildingBlocs Publishing, Inc**

Attn: Aaron B. Kershaw
www.BuildingBlocs.org
www.BuildingBlocsAcademy.com

# Licensing & Usage Disclaimer

**This manual is the intellectual property of BuildingBlocs Literacy LLC and is protected under U.S. and international copyright law.**

This digital edition is intended solely for **administrative, evaluative, and leadership review purposes**. It may be used by institutions, therapists, or organizations to assess alignment with their programming or leadership goals.

## Unauthorized Use Prohibited

The systems described herein, including but not limited to:

- Tiered certification tracks (T1–T6)
- Check-In, Reset, Red Flag™ tools
- Mentor/facilitator/director role structures
- Certification rubrics, pacing models, and LMS structures
- Participant workbooks, coaching guides, or fidelity tools

…are the **protected operational property** of BuildingBlocs Literacy LLC and the BRIGHTPath™ Academy.

**Reproduction, facilitation, training delivery, implementation, or public sharing of this system or its components, whether partial or in full, without a licensing agreement is strictly prohibited.**

## Implementation Requires Licensing

To implement, train with, or distribute any portion of the Built from the Inside™ or Pathlight™ systems, you must first obtain:

- An **active licensing agreement**
- Access to the **BuildingBlocs**™ LMS and certification tools
- Official training and approval by BuildingBlocs Literacy LLC or its licensed agents

For licensing inquiries, program demos, or partnership requests, please contact:

**info@ BuildingBlocsAcademy.com**

## General Disclaimer

All BuildingBlocs Literacy LLC materials, including books, curricula, emotional insight tools, and the EMO-PATH™ System, are protected by copyright and may only be used with appropriate training and licensing. These programs are not a substitute for therapy, clinical treatment, or mental health diagnosis. They are designed to support emotional reflection, educational development, and trauma-informed learning environments.

Unauthorized use, reproduction, or distribution is strictly prohibited. Implementation must follow safety-first guidelines and fidelity protocols. Use by individuals or institutions without a formal license and alignment consultation is not permitted.

For licensing or professional use, please contact: info@BuildingBlocs.org
Visit: www.BuildingBlocs.org

## School-Based and Youth SEL Programs

This material is intended to support social-emotional learning and student self-awareness within school or youth development settings. It is not a replacement for counseling, therapeutic services, or clinical mental health support. EMO-PATH™ and related tools must be facilitated by trained educators or support staff under a licensed program agreement.

Use of these tools requires adherence to safety and emotional pacing protocols. No part of this material may be used outside licensed or approved roles.

## Correctional, Reentry, or Justice-Based Programs

The EMO-PATH™ System and BuildingBlocs materials are designed to enhance reflection, accountability, and emotional development in correctional, reentry, and alternative justice settings. These tools are not therapeutic interventions and do not replace clinical treatment, behavioral therapy, or diagnostic services.

They must be used within licensed programs and under facilitator guidance that prioritizes psychological safety and role-appropriate use.

## Community, Mentoring, and Faith-Based Programs

BuildingBlocs content, including emotional check-ins, reflection tools, and coaching prompts, is intended to support insight and growth in mentoring, peer-led, and values-based programs. These are not clinical tools and are not a replacement for therapy, diagnosis, or crisis care.

All facilitators should receive appropriate training and use materials within the guidelines provided by BuildingBlocs Literacy LLC.

## Therapist-Supplemented or Adjunct Use

BuildingBlocs programs may be used by licensed therapists, counselors, or social workers as a supplement tool, not a replacement for therapy. These tools can enhance insight and track emotional development but are not designed to assess, diagnose, or treat mental health conditions on their own.

Use within clinical settings must adhere to ethical boundaries and support the client's broader treatment plan.

## Little Talks: Big Feelings, Brave Words

1. **Why Feelings Matter**
   Learning what emotions are and why we all have them.

2. **What Happens When We Don't Talk**
   How bottling up feelings can make things harder.

3. **When Big Emotions Take Over**
   What to do when you feel mad, scared, or out of control.

4. **What to Do With Worry**
   Calming anxious thoughts and knowing who to tell.

5. **I Feel It In My Body**
   How your body gives clues about what feels right or wrong.

6. **Secrets That Feel Heavy**
   Knowing the difference between fun secrets and unsafe ones.

7. **When Adults Break Rules**
   What to do when someone older makes you feel confused or unsafe.

8. **I Don't Like That Voice**
   Trusting your gut when someone's tone or energy feels off.

9. **My Rules, My Bubble**
   Understanding your space and when to say no.

10. **Your Circle of 3**
    Finding three grown-ups who help you feel safe and believed.

## 11. Love Shouldn't Hurt or Scare You

Knowing what safe love looks and feels like.

## 12. Brave Words for Hard Moments

Practicing what to say when something feels wrong.

## 13. When Someone Says "I'm Sorry"

How to know if someone really means it, and what happens next.

## 14. What to Do When You Mess Up

Learning how to fix mistakes and still be kind to yourself.

## 15. You're Not Alone

Remembering there are always people who care, help, and believe you.

# How to Use This Book

Hey there! This book is made just for kids like you, ages 7 to 11, who are learning about feelings, friendships, and how to speak up when something doesn't feel right.

You can read it by yourself, with a grown-up, or even in a group. Some kids like to talk about it after reading. Others like to read quietly first. Either way is great!

Each chapter has:

- A short story or idea to think about

- Fun things to try (like drawing, moving, or talking)

- A tool to help you feel safe, calm, or brave

You can go in order, skip around, or take breaks. You're the boss of your pace.

If you ever get confused or something feels like a really big feeling, that's normal. Just talk to a grown-up you trust. This book is here to help, not to make things harder.

You're not alone. And every time you open these pages, you're taking a step toward being strong, smart, and safe, inside and out.

# A Note to the Grown-Up

Dear Parent, Caregiver, or Supporter,

Thank you for opening this book.

*Little Talks* is designed with emotional safety at its core. It helps children build language around feelings, boundaries, and communication, without overwhelming them or introducing content beyond their stage of development.

This book intentionally avoids anything that could be misused, misunderstood, or manipulated. It cannot be used for grooming or coercion, and it encourages children to always bring in another safe adult when something feels off. If you're reading alongside the *Real Talk* or *Before It Spills* books, even better, this allows the whole family to heal and grow together.

Every page is crafted to invite healing conversation, not forced disclosure. You don't need to be a therapist to support your child's emotional development. Just showing up, staying curious, and being honest about your own learning is more than enough.

We're glad you're here. This is a big step for both of you.

# A Note to the Grown-Up

## Safety First: What to Do If Something Feels Wrong

Hi friend! This is just a quick reminder before we start.

If you ever read something in this book that reminds you of something scary, confusing, or uncomfortable...

**Tell a grown-up you trust.**
This might be:

- Your parent or caregiver

- A teacher

- A school counselor

- A coach

- A trusted aunt, uncle, or neighbor

You don't have to carry hard things alone. Ever. There are people who care, who want to listen, and who know how to help.

And just so you know:
**There are no bad kids.**
Only big feelings. And big stories.

If something has happened to you, or is happening now, that doesn't feel okay, telling someone is a brave and powerful step. This book is here to help you feel strong and safe.

# Introduction for Parents & Grown-Ups

Dear Grown-Up,

This book isn't just for kids, it's for **every adult who wants to raise a safe, self-trusting child** in a complicated world.

These pages don't just teach "body safety." They teach something deeper: how to **notice feelings, speak up when something's wrong, and build trust with the adults around them**, including you.

You'll see questions, drawings, and reflections meant to *spark conversations*. But more importantly, you'll see tools that help your child recognize when something doesn't feel right and **build a team of safe grown-ups**.

This book is **not a replacement for parenting**. It's a guide to make parenting braver, more connected, and more honest.

Please read it alongside your child or read it separately and discuss it together. And if you ever feel uncomfortable with what comes up, that's okay. Growth usually starts there.

This book works best when it makes adults a little nervous, and kids a lot stronger.

With you,
*The Little Talks Team*

# Introduction for Kids

Hey there,

This book is all about **you**, your feelings, your voice, and your superpower: being able to notice when something feels *right*... or *wrong*.

We know the world can be confusing sometimes. Even grown-ups break rules. Even friends make mistakes. But your feelings help you figure out what's okay, and what's not.

In this book, you'll meet big feelings, learn cool ways to calm down, and practice using **brave words**. You'll also get to draw, talk, and maybe ask questions some adults don't always know how to answer. (That's okay. They're still learning too.)

You deserve to feel **safe, strong, and heard**. This book is your tool. Let's go.

You ready?

Let's talk. ✦

# My Brave Words Page ✳️

Hi there, Brave One!
Before we begin, let's set the stage.

This is your page, a special space just for you.

---

### ✏️ My Name:

---

### 💬 3 Brave Words I Want to Use More:

1. _______________________________________________

2. _______________________________________________

3. _______________________________________________

These can be any words that help you feel strong, kind, calm, or proud. (Like: "No," "Help," "Enough," "I matter," "Try," "Listen," or "Love.")

---

### 🎨 My Power Symbol:

Draw a picture that reminds you of how strong or brave you are. It could be an animal, a shape, a superhero, a light, a storm cloud, anything that feels like *you* when you're at your best.

**[Big blank box for drawing]**



You can come back to this page anytime.
Your brave words and symbol can grow with you.

You're already powerful. Let's go!

# Chapter 1: Why Feelings Matter

*Learning what emotions are and why we all have them.*

## Let's Talk About It

Have you ever had a feeling so big it filled up your whole body?

Like wanting to yell for no reason… or cry even when nothing "bad" happened?
Or maybe you felt butterflies in your stomach when something exciting was coming?

That's your body talking. And feelings are the words it uses.

Every person, kid, teen, adult, has feelings.
Not because we're weak.
But because we're human.

Feelings are normal. They're needed.
And even the tough ones are part of your superpower.

## Why Do We Even Have Feelings?

Imagine if you didn't know when something was wrong, or what made you happy, or who made you feel safe.
Feelings help with that.

They're like traffic lights:

- 🚦 **Green** means go, safe, calm, connected

- 🚦 **Yellow** means slow down, nervous, unsure, mixed-up

- 🚦 **Red** means stop, angry, scared, hurt, or not okay

Feelings tell us when something's working...
And when something *isn't*.

They help us:

- Make choices

- Ask for help

- Notice when we're not okay

- Connect with people who care

Even the feelings you don't *like*, they still matter.


## Feelings Can Show Up In:

- Your **body** (tight shoulders, fast heartbeat, shaky hands)

- Your **thoughts** ("Nobody likes me," "I'm gonna mess this up")

- Your **actions** (shutting down, yelling, hiding, laughing too hard)

And you know what?
**All of that is normal.**

You're not "too much."
You're not "too sensitive."
You're just feeling. And that means something is alive in you.


## Pause for a Check-In

Right now, stop and ask yourself:

- "What's one feeling I've had today?"

- "Where do I feel it in my body?"

- "What would I name that feeling if it were a color?"

Let's try this:

| Color | Might Feel Like... |
| --- | --- |
| 💙 Blue | Sad, quiet, tired, or peaceful |
| ❤️ Red | Angry, loud, fast, or fired-up |
| 💛 Yellow | Excited, bouncy, nervous |
| 💚 Green | Calm, safe, chill, okay |
| 🖤 Black | Heavy, stuck, mad-at-everything |
| 🤍 White | Numb, blank, zoned-out, confused |

There's no wrong answer.

And it's okay if your colors mix.

# Try This Tool: My Color of the Day

1. Close your eyes.

2. Think about your body, your mind, your day.

3. Pick your color.

4. Ask yourself:

- Do I like how this color feels?

- Do I want to keep it or change it?

- What could help me shift it, just a little?

**Bonus:** Tell someone your color. You don't have to explain it.

Just say it.

That's being brave with your truth.

## Journal Time:

Write or draw your answers to one (or all) of these:

- One feeling I have a lot but don't talk about is: ___________

- When I feel that way, my body: _______________________________

- I wish people knew that when I act like _____, I really feel _____.

No pressure. No rules.
This is your space.


## Big Reminder

Feelings aren't bad.
They're messengers.
They don't need to be hidden, fixed, or feared.

They just need you to *listen*.

That's the start of being your own safe place.

# Chapter 2: What Happens When We Don't Talk

*How bottling up feelings can make things harder.*

## Let's Talk About It

Have you ever tried to hold in a laugh until your belly hurt?
Or stayed quiet when something made you mad, even though your heart was pounding?

Sometimes, we keep our feelings locked up tight.
We might do it to stay out of trouble.
Or to not seem "dramatic."
Or because we're not sure who's safe to talk to.

But here's the truth:

**Feelings that don't come out still find a way out.**

They can show up in ways we don't expect, like stomachaches, yelling, being mean, crying for no reason, or wanting to be alone all the time.

## The Soda Bottle Trick

Imagine your feelings are like bubbles in a soda bottle.
Every time something happens, someone yells, you feel left out, you get scared, more bubbles get shaken up inside.

If you never twist the cap to let some of the pressure out?
**POP.**

Boom. Mess everywhere.

Talking is like slowly opening the cap.
It lets the pressure out before you explode.

## Why We Sometimes Stay Silent

There are lots of reasons kids don't talk about feelings.
And none of them make you weak.

- "No one will understand."

- "What if they get mad?"

- "I don't want to cry."

- "They'll say I'm too sensitive."

- "I don't even know what I feel."

Sound familiar?

You're not alone.
Even adults do this.

But staying silent doesn't make the feelings disappear.
It just makes them *heavier*.

## What Bottled-Up Feelings Might Look Like

- Getting mad at small things

- Not wanting to eat or sleep

- Headaches, tummy trouble

- Saying "I'm fine" when you're not

- Being mean without knowing why

- Feeling "numb" or like you don't care about anything

It's not about being bad.
It's about needing somewhere for the feelings to go.

## Try This Tool: The Steam Valve

Grab a notebook, a paper, or just a quiet moment.

Answer one of these steam-release questions:

- "What's something I didn't say today that I wish I had?"

- "Is there a feeling I've been pushing down?"

- "If my body could talk, what would it say?"

You don't need to show it to anyone.
But if you want to, pick a safe adult to read it with.

This is how we *let pressure out*, so it doesn't build up inside.

## Journal Time:

Try finishing one (or more) of these sentences:

- "One thing I've been holding in is…"

- "When I stay quiet too long, I start to feel…"

- "I wish I could tell someone that…"

You don't have to share it right away.
But every time you write or speak a little truth, the bottle gets lighter.


## Big Reminder

**Talking doesn't make you weak. It makes space.**

Space to breathe.
Space to heal.
Space for someone to meet you there.

Your voice matters, even when it's just a whisper.

# Chapter 3: When Big Emotions Take Over

*What to do when you feel mad, scared, or out of control.*

## Let's Talk About It

Sometimes emotions sneak up like ninjas.
Other times, they crash in like a wave.

One minute you're fine.
The next, BOOM. You're yelling, crying, hiding, or shaking.

That's called a **big feeling moment**.

And even if you feel out of control, you're not broken.
You're just overwhelmed. And there are ways to come back to calm.

## What Big Feelings Can Look Like

- Yelling or hitting

- Crying and not knowing why

- Hiding under a blanket or behind a door

- Running away or freezing

- Saying things you don't mean

- Feeling like your heart is racing or your hands won't stop moving

When this happens, it's not about being "bad."
It means your **feelings are louder than your calm**.
And we all need help finding our calm again.


## What's Going On Inside

When a big emotion hits, like anger, fear, or panic, your brain sends a message to protect you.
That's called "fight, flight, or freeze."

It's like a fire alarm going off in your body:
🚨 "Run!"
🚨 "Fight back!"
🚨 "Hide!"

But not every big feeling is a fire.
Sometimes it's just a feeling that needs a place to land.

## Try This Tool: The 3-Breath Reset

When a big emotion shows up, you can hit the **Reset Button** with three simple breaths.

**Step 1: Ground Your Body**
Sit down or press your feet into the floor. Put your hand on your chest or belly.

**Step 2: Breathe In… and Out…**
Breathe in through your nose for 4 seconds.
Hold for 2.
Breathe out through your mouth for 6 seconds.
Repeat 3 times.

**Step 3: Say Something Kind**
Say in your head:
"I'm safe. I can slow down. I don't have to fix everything right now."

Even if the feeling is still there, the panic starts to shrink.


## Journal Time:

- A big feeling I had recently was…

- I felt it in my ___________.

- One thing that helped (or could've helped) me calm down was…

Drawing it out helps too, make a "Feelings Volcano" or a "Calm Island" if you want!

## Big Reminder

Big emotions don't make you dangerous.
They make you **human**.
And humans can learn how to slow down, get help, and feel better.

You're not too much.
You're just feeling deeply. And that's okay.

# Chapter 4: What to Do With Worry

*Calming anxious thoughts and knowing who to tell.*

**Let's Talk About It**

Worry is a tricky feeling.
It can whisper small questions...
*"What if I mess up?"*
*"What if something bad happens?"*
*"What if they don't like me?"*

Or it can shout loud thoughts you can't turn off.
Even when nothing is wrong on the outside, worry makes your brain and body feel like everything is wrong on the inside.

But here's something powerful:

**Worry doesn't mean danger.**
It means your brain is trying to protect you.
And you can learn how to answer it.

## What Worry Feels Like

- Tight chest or belly

- Can't sit still

- Feeling sick or dizzy

- Thinking the same thing over and over

- Scared to try something new

- Wanting to avoid people, places, or stuff

Worry grows in quiet.
But it shrinks when it's named and shared.

## Try This Tool: Name It, Tame It, Talk It

You don't have to fight worry. You just need to talk to it.

**Step 1: Name It**
Say, "This feeling is worry. It's just trying to help, but it's being really loud."

**Step 2: Tame It**
Breathe in slowly. Let your shoulders drop. Wiggle your fingers. Remind your body it's not in danger.

**Step 3: Talk It Out**
Find a grown-up you trust and say:
"Something's bugging me and I want to tell you."
You don't have to explain it perfectly. You just have to begin.

## Safe Adults to Tell

- A parent or step-parent

- A teacher or school counselor

- A coach or group leader

- A grandparent or family friend

- A therapist or helper person

It's okay to keep trying until someone listens.
You deserve to be heard.

## Journal Time:

- A worry that keeps showing up for me is…

- One thing I want to understand better is…

- When I talk about my worries, I feel ___________.

You can draw your worry as a character too. What does it look like? What silly name could you give it?

## Big Reminder

Worry doesn't mean you're weak.
It means your heart is trying to stay safe.
But you don't have to do it alone.

You are not your worries.
You are brave enough to face them.

# Chapter 5: I Feel It In My Body

*How your body gives clues about what feels right or wrong.*

## Let's Talk About It

Your body is smart, even when your brain is confused.

It sends messages all day long.

When you're excited, you might feel butterflies.

When you're nervous, your tummy might flip.

When something's *not okay*, your body often knows first.

That's called your **body signal**.

And learning to listen to it can keep you safe, calm, and strong.

## Body Clues to Notice

Let's say you walk into a room and your body suddenly feels:

- Tight in your chest
- Like you want to run
- Shaky or frozen
- Like your stomach is in knots
- Like you want to yell, hide, or cry
- Like something just feels "off"

That doesn't always mean something bad is happening.
But it *does* mean your body is trying to talk to you.

It's saying:
**"Hey. Pause. Pay attention. Something doesn't feel right."**

## Try This Tool: Body Scan Pause

Take a minute to notice what your body is saying.

1. Sit or lie down comfortably.

2. Close your eyes (or keep them open, your choice).

3. Imagine a flashlight slowly scanning from your head to your toes.

4. Ask yourself:

   - What feels tight?
   - What feels heavy or jumpy?
   - What feels calm or soft?

You don't have to change anything. Just notice it.
Your body is giving clues. And clues help you stay connected.

## he "Green, Yellow, Red" Check

Think of your body like a traffic light:

- 🟢 **Green** – I feel calm, safe, okay
- 🟡 **Yellow** – Something feels a little weird or off
- 🔴 **Red** – Something feels wrong, scary, or unsafe

If you're in yellow or red, that's a great time to **pause**, **breathe**, and **talk to a safe adult**.

## Journal Time:

- My body feels calm when…
- I feel "yellow light" when…
- One time my body told me something important was…

You can draw your traffic light body too, green at the top, yellow in the middle, red at the bottom. What parts light up for you?

## Big Reminder

Your body is not too sensitive.
It's not lying.
It's your built-in radar, and it's trying to help.

When you learn to hear it, you learn to help *yourself*.

# Chapter 6: Secrets That Feel Heavy

*Knowing the difference between fun secrets and unsafe ones.*

## Let's Talk About It

Some secrets feel light and fun.
Like a birthday surprise.
Or a whispered plan to make your teacher smile.

Other secrets feel heavy.
Like a rock in your chest.
They might come with words like:
*"Don't tell anyone."*
*"This is just between us."*
*"If you say something, you'll get in trouble."*

Let's be clear:
**If a secret makes you feel scared, weird, or confused, it's not your job to keep it.**

## What Heavy Secrets Feel Like

- Feeling nervous or scared after someone tells you something

- Being told not to tell an adult

- Feeling like you might get in trouble if you speak up

- Thinking about it over and over, even when you don't want to

- Feeling sad, stuck, or sick when you remember it

Safe secrets make you feel excited or kind.
Unsafe ones feel like they're **trapping you.**


## Try This Tool: The Secret Test

When someone tells you a secret, ask yourself:

1. **Is it kind or sneaky?**
   Does it make you feel happy or scared?

2. **Would I be okay if a trusted adult knew?**
   If not, it might be a secret that shouldn't stay secret.

3. **Is someone getting hurt or scared by this secret?**
   Then it needs to be shared with someone safe.

## You Can Always Tell

If a secret feels heavy or confusing, here's what you do:

- Go to a grown-up you trust (parent, teacher, counselor, coach).
- Say: *"I was told something and it feels heavy. I need help."*

You don't have to explain it perfectly.
You don't have to fix it yourself.
**You just have to speak up.**

## Journal Time:

- A safe secret might be...
- A heavy secret might feel like...
- One grown-up I trust enough to tell is...

Draw a "Secret Backpack", what kind of secrets feel light to carry? What ones feel too heavy?

## Big Reminder

Some people use secrets to hide bad choices.
But you don't have to carry those secrets.

**Safe grown-ups want to help.**
If someone told you something that feels wrong, you're not a tattletale.
You're a truth-teller. And truth helps keep people safe.

# Chapter 7: When Adults Break Rules

*What to do when someone older makes you feel confused or unsafe.*

## Let's Talk About It

Most adults try their best to take care of kids, teach them things, and keep them safe.
But sometimes, adults break rules.
Not the silly ones, like eating dessert first.
We're talking about **the big rules** that protect people.

Like:

- Respecting your body and your space

- Using kind words, not scary ones

- Telling the truth

- Keeping kids safe, not scared

If an adult breaks those kinds of rules, **that is not your fault.** And you're allowed to tell someone, even if that adult told you not to.

## How It Might Feel

When an adult crosses a line, you might:

- Feel scared or frozen

- Have a funny or yucky feeling in your belly

- Start avoiding that person

- Feel confused because they're nice *sometimes*

- Think you'll get in trouble if you say anything

- Feel like no one would believe you

But here's the truth:
**It is never your job to protect an adult who's hurting you.**
Even if they say it's "a secret."
Even if they say you "asked for it."
Even if they're someone you love.

## Try This Tool: The Grown-Up Rule Check

If you're not sure whether something is okay, ask yourself:

1. **Does it make me feel weird, scared, or confused inside?**

2. **Did the adult tell me to keep it secret?**

3.  **Would I be scared if my other safe grown-ups found out?**

4.  **Did they say something like "this is just our special thing"?**

If you said yes to any of those...
**Tell. A. Safe. Grown-Up.**
Right away.

## What To Say and Do

You can say:

- *"Something happened and it doesn't feel okay."*

- *"I need help with something a grown-up did."*

- *"This is hard to talk about, but I want to tell."*

You can write it down or draw it if talking is too hard.
You can ask a safe adult to help you call someone else if needed.

You can also call or text a help line for kids.
You are never alone.

## Journal Time:

- I feel safe when adults...

- If an adult broke a rule that hurt someone, I would...

- One thing I know is true about my safety is...

You can also draw a "Safety Shield." Inside the shield, draw people, words, or tools that help you feel safe and brave.

## Big Reminder

**No adult should ever make you feel scared, ashamed, or trapped.**
Even if it's someone close to you.
Even if they say you won't be believed.

Your job is to be a kid.
**Their job is to keep you safe.**
If they don't... it's time to tell someone who will.

# Chapter 8: I Don't Like That Voice

*Trusting your gut when someone's tone or energy feels off.*

## Let's Talk About It

Sometimes it's not the words that feel weird, it's the way they're said.
A person might be **smiling**, but their voice feels scary.
They might say something **nice**, but your belly flips like it knows something's wrong.
That feeling matters.

It's called your **gut feeling** or **inner voice**.
And it's one of the most powerful tools you've got.

## What "Off" Feels Like

You might notice:

- A strange tone that feels mean, even if the words are polite

- A too-nice voice that gives you the ick

- Jokes that feel more like warnings

- A look that makes you shrink or freeze

- Pressure that's hidden under "friendly" talk

Even if it's confusing, **you don't have to explain why it feels wrong.**
You're allowed to notice.
You're allowed to say no.
You're allowed to get away from it.


## Try This Tool: Voice Vibes Check

When someone talks to you and your body reacts, ask:

1. **Does my chest feel tight?**

2. **Do I feel frozen, even if I want to move?**

3. **Does my stomach feel weird or twisty?**

4. **Would I feel better if someone else were here with me?**

If you say "yes" to one or more of these...
That voice or tone may not be safe.

## What You Can Say

Here are some things you can say if someone's voice or energy makes you uncomfortable:

- *"I don't like that."*

- *"Please stop talking to me like that."*

- *"I need space."*

- *"I'm going to go now."*

And then... tell someone safe.
Even if nothing *bad* happened, your body was trying to say something.
And that means it matters.


## Journal Time:

- A voice I love to hear is...

- One time I got the "uh-oh" feeling from someone's voice or tone was...

- When I trust my gut, I feel...

You can draw two faces, one that makes you feel cozy and calm, and one that gives you the "uh-ohs." What's different between them?

## Big Reminder

**Your feelings are your guide.**

Not every weird voice is dangerous, but *every time* you get that "hmm…" feeling, you get to pause and check in.

You're not too sensitive.
You're just learning to trust yourself.
And that's a superpower.

**Your feelings are your guide.**

# Chapter 9: My Rules, My Bubble

*Understanding your space and when to say no.*

## Let's Talk About It

Every person has an invisible **bubble** around them.
This bubble is made of your body, your feelings, and your comfort.
And guess what?
**You get to decide who steps inside.**

It doesn't matter if it's a friend, a grown-up, or someone you love.
If something feels wrong or too close, you can say:
**"That's not okay with me."**

You don't need a reason.
You don't need permission.
You already have the right.

## What Boundaries Look Like

Boundaries are like the rules you set for your bubble.
They might sound like:

- "I don't want a hug right now."

- "Please knock before coming in."

- "That game makes me uncomfortable."

- "I don't like being tickled."

- "Stop. That's not funny to me."

Some people will respect your bubble.
Others might get mad, confused, or laugh.
But that doesn't mean you're wrong.
**It means you're being brave.**


## Try This Tool: The Bubble Map

Draw a circle. That's your bubble.

Inside the circle, write or draw:

- Things you like

- Things you're okay with

- Things you don't like

- People you trust to respect your bubble

Use color or symbols to show what feels good and what feels "too much."

## Words That Protect Your Bubble

You can say:

- "I'm not comfortable with that."

- "Please don't do that again."

- "I need space."

- "I said no. Please respect that."

If someone keeps crossing your line, **tell a grown-up you trust.** No one, even a friend or family member, has the right to break your bubble rules.

## Journal Time:

- One bubble rule I have is…

- A time I felt someone respected my space was…

- A time I wish I'd said something is…

You can also draw your bubble like a shield, what symbols or shapes protect it?

## Big Reminder

Boundaries aren't mean. They're healthy.
They help people understand how to treat you with care and respect.

You are allowed to say **no**.

You are allowed to change your mind.

You are allowed to protect your space, always.

# Chapter 10: Your Circle of 3

*Finding three grown-ups who help you feel safe and believed.*

## Let's Talk About It

Everyone needs a **Circle of 3**, three grown-ups you can count on.

These are your safety people.

They listen. They believe you.

They help you when things feel big or confusing.

You don't need to have the *perfect* words.

You don't need to explain everything.

You just need to know who to go to when something doesn't feel right.

## What Makes Someone "Safe"?

A safe grown-up:

- Listens without getting mad or scary

- Believes you, even if it's hard to hear

- Helps you solve problems without blame

- Doesn't keep unsafe secrets

- Makes you feel more calm, not more confused

It might be:

- A parent or step-parent

- A teacher or school counselor

- An aunt, uncle, grandparent, or godparent

- A coach, pastor, or family friend

You get to choose.
It's your circle.


## Try This Tool: The Circle of 3 Drawing

1. Draw a circle.

2. Inside the circle, write the names of three grown-ups who help you feel safe.

3.  Around the circle, write what each person helps you with (e.g., listens, hugs, helps talk to other adults, prays with me).

4.  If you're not sure who to pick yet, that's okay. Write who you *might* want to talk to or who you'd *like* to feel safer with.

This is your team. You can add or change names anytime.

## What You Can Say to Them

If something feels scary, weird, or wrong, you can say:

- "Can I tell you something hard?"
- "I need help figuring something out."
- "Something happened, and I don't know what to do."

Or just:

- "Can we talk?"

Your Circle of 3 doesn't need all the answers.
They just need to **listen** and **care**.
And you deserve that.

## Journal Time:

- The people who make me feel safe are...
- I feel believed when...
- A grown-up I'd like to trust more is...

You can draw each person with a symbol (heart, light, shield) to show how they help.



## Big Reminder

You don't have to go through hard stuff alone.
Even if someone tries to make you feel small, your Circle of 3 can help you feel strong again.

Choosing your people is like building your own team of superheroes.

# Chapter 11: Love Shouldn't Hurt or Scare You

*Knowing what safe love looks and feels like.*

## Let's Talk About It

Love is supposed to feel warm, kind, and safe.
But sometimes, people say "I love you" and then act in ways that feel scary, loud, or confusing.

That's not what love is supposed to be.

**Love doesn't yell to scare.**
**Love doesn't hit to teach.**
**Love doesn't ask you to stay quiet about something that hurts.**

Even grown-ups can get love wrong.
But you don't have to believe love should feel bad.

# What Safe Love Looks Like

Love can look like:

- A hug that you *want*

- Listening when you're upset

- Saying sorry when someone messes up

- Letting you be yourself

- Protecting your feelings, not hurting them

Love does **not** look like:

- Threats or scary words

- Touches that make you freeze or cry

- Being blamed for someone else's anger

- Being told to keep secrets that feel bad

- Feeling afraid in your own home

If love hurts or confuses you, it's not your fault.
It's okay to speak up, even if it's someone close to you.

# Try This Tool: Love Check-In

Fill in the blanks or talk them out with a safe person:

- Love feels safe when __________

- Love feels scary when __________

- I feel most loved when __________

- Someone once made me feel scared, and I wish they
  ________

You can draw a heart and color the parts that feel warm, and the parts that feel heavy.

## What You Can Say

If someone says "I love you," but it doesn't feel good, you can say:

- "That doesn't feel like love to me."

- "Please don't talk to me like that."

- "I need to tell someone about this."

Love should never be a secret that hurts.
Love should never make you feel small.

## Journal Time:

- What I've learned about love is...

- One way I show love that feels safe is...

- A time love didn't feel good was...

You're allowed to question what love means.
You're allowed to want better.

## Big Reminder

Just because someone says "I love you" doesn't mean they're loving you in a safe way.
**Love is supposed to help you feel strong, not scared.**

You deserve love that is patient, kind, and true.
And it's okay to speak up if that's not what you're getting.

## Big Reminder

# Chapter 12: Brave Words for Hard Moments

*Practicing what to say when something feels wrong.*

## Let's Talk About It

Sometimes your heart knows something's off...
But your mouth gets stuck.
You might freeze.
You might smile even though you feel scared.
You might go quiet when you want to shout.

That's okay.

Big feelings can make words hard to find.
That's why we practice **Brave Words** ahead of time.

Brave Words help you speak up when something isn't okay.
They don't have to be loud.
They just have to be **true**.

## When to Use Brave Words

Use Brave Words when:

- Someone crosses your body boundary

- A secret feels heavy or wrong

- You're being blamed for something you didn't do

- You're feeling unsafe, confused, or scared

- You need help and don't know how to ask

You don't have to explain everything.
You don't have to be perfect.
You just have to **speak**.

## Try This Tool: Say It, Try It, Own It

Practice in three steps:

1. **Say It** – Read one of the Brave Words lines below.

2. **Try It** – Say it out loud to yourself or with someone you trust.

3. **Own It** – Imagine using that sentence in a real moment. What does it feel like?

**Examples of Brave Words**:

- "Stop. I don't like that."

- "That made me uncomfortable."

- "I don't want to be touched like that."

- "This feels wrong and I want to tell someone."

- "I need help."

- "I'm not okay with this."

- "Please back up."

- "No."

Short. Strong. Yours.

## Practice Time:

Take turns practicing with someone you trust:

- They say a sentence (like, "It's just a secret between us!")

- You answer with a Brave Word that feels right.

Make it a game. Switch roles. Laugh if it helps.
But always come back to your power: **your voice.**

## Journal Time:

- One Brave Word I want to remember is:

- A time I wish I had spoken up was:

- Next time, I will try to say:

You can write your Brave Words on a card or paper and keep it somewhere special.

## Big Reminder

Brave Words don't mean you're rude.
They mean you're **ready**.
They mean you've practiced.
And they mean you know your worth.

You don't have to be big to be brave.
Just honest.

# Chapter 13: When Someone Says "I'm Sorry"

*How to know if someone really means it, and what happens next.*

## Let's Talk About It

Everyone makes mistakes.
Sometimes people hurt us, on purpose or by accident.
And sometimes, they say "I'm sorry."

But not all "I'm sorrys" are the same.

Some are **real**.
Some are **just words**.
Some come with change.
Some come with more hurt.

You get to notice how it feels in your body.
You get to decide what feels safe for you.

## What Makes a Real Apology?

A real "I'm sorry" looks like:

- Saying what they did wrong ("I yelled, and that was scary.")

- Not blaming you ("You made me mad" isn't an apology.)

- Changing the behavior, not just saying sorry again

- Giving you space if you need it

- Trying to earn your trust back slowly

A fake "I'm sorry" might feel:

- Rushed

- Pressured

- Like you have to forgive right away

- Like the same hurt keeps happening

**You never have to accept an apology that doesn't feel true.**

## Try This Tool: The Apology Test

Think about a time someone said "I'm sorry."
Ask yourself:

1. Did they name what they did wrong?

2. Did they stop doing it after they said sorry?

3. Did they seem to care how I felt?

4. Did they try to make things better without blaming me?

5. Did I feel safe around them afterward?

If most answers are "yes," that's a real apology.
If not, it might be time to ask for help.


## What You Can Say

When someone says sorry and you're not ready:

- "I need time to think."

- "Thanks for saying that. I still feel hurt."

- "I hear you, but I need you to show me you mean it."

- "I don't feel ready to talk yet."

You're allowed to **forgive slowly**.
You're allowed to **not forgive** if it's not safe.


## Journal Time:

- A time someone said "I'm sorry" to me was…

- I felt safe/unsafe because…

- One way I know someone is really sorry is…

You can draw two hearts, one that feels safe, one that feels unsure.
Label what each needs.

## Big Reminder

An apology is a **first step**, not the whole path.

It's okay to hope someone means it.

It's also okay to protect your peace while you wait and see.

Real love owns mistakes.

Real safety feels different after "I'm sorry."

# Chapter 14: What to Do When You Mess Up

*Learning how to fix mistakes and still be kind to yourself.*

## Let's Talk About It

Everybody messes up.
Sometimes you say something mean.
Sometimes you break a rule.
Sometimes you let big feelings take over.

That doesn't make you a bad kid.
It makes you human.

The important part is what you do **next**.

Do you hide it?
Blame someone else?
Get mad at yourself?

Or do you take a breath, tell the truth, and try to make things right?

## What Owning It Looks Like

When you mess up, try these steps:

1. **Pause and breathe.**
   Let your body calm down before you speak.

2. **Tell the truth.**
   Say what really happened. No blaming.

3. **Say sorry with action.**
   "I'm sorry" is good.
   Changing the behavior is better.

4. **Fix what you can.**
   Clean it up. Help out. Write a note. Show effort.

5. **Be kind to yourself.**
   You're growing. You're learning. That matters most.

## Try This Tool: The Fix-It Five

Write these out or say them aloud when you need to repair:

1. What did I do?

2. Who did it hurt or upset?

3. How do I think they felt?

4. What can I do to make it better?

5. What will I do differently next time?

These steps help you move forward, not stay stuck.

## What You Can Say

Here are words to use when you want to make things right:

- "I messed up, and I want to fix it."
- "I'm sorry I hurt you. I see that now."
- "Next time, I'll do _____ instead."
- "I still care, even though I made a mistake."

You don't have to wait for someone to forgive you.
Doing the right thing feels good on the inside.

## Journal Time:

- A time I messed up and learned something:
- One thing I wish I had done differently:
- Something I can do next time to stay calm:

Draw a "Restart Button." What helps you feel ready to try again?

## Big Reminder

Mistakes don't mean you're bad.
They mean you're learning how to be better.

Every time you choose honesty, kindness, and growth, you're being brave.

Say it with me:
**"I can make mistakes and still be a good kid."**

# Chapter 15: You're Not Alone

*Remembering there are always people who care, help, and believe you.*

## Let's Talk About It

Sometimes, big feelings feel like a storm.
And storms can make you feel small.
Like you're the only one going through it.

But guess what?

**You're not the only one.**
You're not alone.
You're not too much.
And you're not invisible.

There are people, right now, who care.
Even when it's hard to feel it.

## Who's in Your Corner?

You might have:

- A parent who's learning to listen better

- A teacher who smiles when you walk in

- A counselor who always keeps your secrets safe

- A neighbor who checks in

- A coach who believes in second chances

- A sibling who gets it

- A friend who sees the real you

Even one safe person can make all the difference.

You don't need to have all the answers.
You just need someone who'll sit with you while you find them.


## Try This Tool: The Helper Map

Draw a circle in the middle of a page with your name in it.
Then add:

- People who help you feel seen

- People who listen without judging

- People who make you laugh or feel strong

- People who make you feel safe when you're scared

No one has a perfect team.
But everyone deserves one.

## What You Can Say

When you need help:

- "I don't know what I feel, but I need someone."

- "Can you just sit with me for a minute?"

- "I think I need help with something big."

- "This feels hard to say, but I want to tell you something."

You don't have to yell.
You don't have to be perfect.
You just have to be real.


## Journal Time:

- Someone I trust is...

- I feel safe when...

- One thing I want a grown-up to know is...

Draw a "Safe Space" , this could be a real place, a person's arms, or even a feeling.


## Big Reminder

You don't have to do this life alone.
You don't have to hold all the feelings, all the time.

Asking for help is brave.
Being honest is strong.
**You are never alone, even when it feels like it.**

That's the end of this book, but not the end of your story.

You're part of a team now.
A team that sees you, hears you, and walks beside you.

Keep talking. Keep feeling. Keep growing.
We're right here with you. 💛

# You Finished *Little Talks*!

*That's a big deal.*

You just did something brave.
You read a whole book that talked about big feelings, hard things, and how to speak your truth.

That takes guts.

You might still have questions. That's okay.
You might want to go back and read parts again. Also okay.
You might feel a little stronger than you did before. That's **amazing**.

## Here's What to Remember:

- **Your feelings matter.**

- **You are allowed to say no.**

- **It's okay to ask for help.**

- **You don't have to figure it all out alone.**

## Want to Keep Going?

This book is part of a family series.
If you're reading with a grown-up, they might have *Before It Spills* (for them) or *Real Talk* (for teens).

Those books have some of the same tools, stories, and lessons, just told in ways that fit their age.
It's how we grow together, not apart.

## One Last Thing...

Take a minute and write down three things you learned or felt:

1. ______________________________________________

2. ______________________________________________

3. ______________________________________________

Now say this to yourself:

**"I am growing. I am strong. And I am never alone."**


You're part of a brave, honest team now.
We're proud of you.

🧡 Keep talking. Keep feeling. Keep showing up. 🧡

# About the Author

**Aaron B. Kershaw** is a father of 4, mentor, Marine veteran, and trauma-informed educator who knows firsthand what it means to break cycles and build legacy. Drawing from decades of lived experience, Aaron writes with a rare blend of grit, grace, and grounded truth that resonates across generations.

He's spent his life working in rooms that hold both pain and potential; from youth mentorship programs and family counseling spaces to churches seeking healing beyond the altar. As the founder of *The BrightPath Academy* and *BuildingBlocs Literacy*, Aaron helps families and communities navigate emotional healing with courage, faith, and practical tools.

Aaron doesn't write as an expert in theory; he writes as someone who's been there. A parent who's yelled and regretted it. A son who grew up too fast. A man who had to learn emotional regulation in real time, with real stakes. His work is a mirror, a map, and a gentle nudge forward for those ready to reset what family means.

**The Family Reset Series** is not just a curriculum. It's a calling. And Aaron's mission is simple:
To help families speak truth, show up fully, and heal together; one honest conversation at a time.

9 7989 03 450299